Salvation Through Jesus Christ

Poems and Verse

Scripture taken from the HOLY BIBLE, NEW INTERNATIONAL VERSION, NIV, Copyright c 1973 1978, 1984 by International Bible Society. Used by Permission of Zondervan. All rights reserved worldwide.

Copyright © 2024 Sandy Bohon LMHC

All rights reserved. This book or any portion thereof may not be reproduced or used in any manner whatsoever without the express written permission of the publisher except for the use of brief quotations in a book review.

ISBN-13: 979-8-9904016-0-0

Christ is the Only Way

Life on this earth is short
And it is where we will decide
Where we will spend eternity,
Will we in heaven abide?

Christ died on the cross for our sin
And He is the only way
That we can enter heaven
When we all die one day.

So, do not trust in yourselves,
Or any good deed you may do
Nor any amount of money
Can ever help save you.

Have you ever thought about eternal life, and where you will be going when you die? The Bible teaches us that salvation is through Jesus Christ.

"For God so loved the world that He gave His one and only Son, that whoever believes in Him shall not perish but have eternal life." John 3:16

At the Well

Jesus came to the well to drink,
    And there a woman He met,
His disciples left Him there
    For to town some food to get.

Jesus asked her for a drink,
    The woman questioned Him why,
Jesus said if you drink from Me
    Then you will never die.

Jesus is the living water
    That springs to eternal life,
One drink from Him is all we need
    To receive true afterlife.

Jesus Christ gives eternal life to those who put their trust in Him as their Savior.

"Jesus answered, 'Everyone who drinks this water will be thirsty again, but whoever drinks the water I give them will never thirst. Indeed, the water I give them will become in them a spring of water welling up to eternal life.'" John 4:13,14

God Knows Our Ways

Looking at the stars at night
    Makes me think of God above,
Who spoke them into creation,
    And He also sends His love.

Why would He love a worm like me
    Who has fallen over again,
I try so hard to be good
    Then somehow sins slip in.

So, I'll take God at His word
    It's what the Bible says,
That God loves each of us
    And knows all of our ways.

We have all done something wrong and sinned, and God knows this. God loves us in spite of our sins.

"For all have sinned and fall short of the glory of God." Romans 3:23

At Calvary

As leaves falling in the breeze
    And softly hit the ground,
When my life on earth is over
    My soul is heaven bound.

Not because I've been good,
    But my life in Christ I place
Who died for me on Calvary,
    And saved me by His grace.

Living a good life, prayers, or reading the Bible cannot get us into heaven. Salvation is a free gift from God through Jesus Christ.

"For it is by grace you have been saved, through faith - and this is not from yourselves, it is the gift of God, not by works, so that no one can boast." Ephesians 2:8,9

Double Vision

Along this life we travel through
    Light and dark are all around,
Evil wants to ensnare you
    Beating a deafening sound.

Through foggy mist we can't see
    All the good that blends with sin,
Mixing dark with reality,
    We call this double vision.

Through the mist we see a light
    It is Jesus shining in,
Only He can restore your sight,
    And give you single vision.

There are many religions and beliefs in the world and it can be confusing as to which is the correct one. God is calling out to everyone to trust Christ as their Savior.

"When Jesus spoke again to the people, He said, 'I am the light of the world. Whoever follows Me will never walk in darkness, but will have the light of life.'" John 8:14

Lost Doll

I saw a baby doll
   Lying along the way,
Which a little girl could,
   No longer with it play.

Is it her favorite doll
   And she'll miss it very much?
Or something she threw away,
   My thoughts go on as such.

As in life we lose things
   That will never again be found,
While other things are useless,
   And just left upon the ground.

When you trust Christ as your Savior you are born into the family of God and become a child of God. God loves us and never kicks us out of His family. You cannot lose your salvation.

"All that the Father gives Me will come to Me, and whoever comes to Me I will never drive away. And this is the will of Him who sent Me, that I shall lose none of all of those He has given me, but raise them up at the last day."
John 6:37,39

Life is a Vapor

Our life is like a vapor
A flower that fades away,
A sunset in the evening
That closes off the day.

What purpose is our life
As fleeting as the wind?
What advice to give others,
As echoes in the mind.

But just as Nicodemus
Sought out Jesus in the night
And asked about salvation
To end his anguished plight.

Trust Christ as your Savior
So, when this life is past,
We can spend eternity
In heaven that will last.

Sometimes people feel that they don't have any reason for living and life seems pointless. God is the one who gives us purpose and a reason for living.

"Trust in the Lord with all your heart and lean not on your own understanding; in all your ways submit to Him, and He will make your paths straight." Proverbs 3:5,6

Peace to All

I saw a duck swimming by
    The moon was just a sliver,
Birds were flying in the air
    As I sat beside the river.

The first star was shining
    As darkness covered the air,
The glory of God was bringing
    Peace to all everywhere.

God created the heavens and earth for us to enjoy. God also wants to have a relationship with each of us and wants to be a part of our lives. We can have fellowship with Him when we trust Christ as our Savior.

"You alone are the Lord. You made the heavens, even the highest heavens, and all their starry host, the earth and all that is on it, the seas and all that is in them. You give life to everything, and the multitudes of heaven worship you." Nehemiah 9:6

Life is Brief

Our life is like a vapor
    A brief moment in time,
In God's sea of eternity,
    A moment so sublime.

Like an autumn leaf swirling
    Up high and floating low,
Falling to the distant ground
    To disappear below.

Even though this life is brief
    God wants us all to be,
With Christ who paid for our sin,
    For all eternity.

Life is brief and eternity is forever. If you trust Christ as your Savior, you can know that you will spend eternity with Christ.

"I write these things to you who believe in the name of the Son of God so that you may know that you have eternal life." 1 John 5:13

The Lord is My Shepherd

The Lord is my Shepherd, I shall not want,
But we are His sheep and continue to stray.
The wolves come along to scatter us out
And upon the weak they will pounce and prey.
Christ will lead us upon the green pastures,
But we are rebellious and go our own way.
In the shadow of death, we will have no fear,
But we are fearful and anxious throughout the day.
Arguing, lying, and deceit are among us,
Unrest and turmoil is in our work and play.

Jesus the good Shepherd is calling us still,
For us to trust in Him and to change our way.
He is calling us to fellowship with Him,
Beside the still waters He wants us to lay.
My stubborn heart finally let His love shine in,
Now I will praise Him throughout all my day.

The Lord is my Shepherd, I shall not want.

Jesus is calling us to come to Him so he can take care of us and guide us. He is the good Shepherd.

Psalm 23

The Lord is my Shepherd, I lack nothing. He makes me lie down in green pastures, He leads me beside quiet waters, He refreshes my soul. He guides me along the right paths for His name's sake. Even though I walk through the darkest valley, I will fear no evil, for You are with me: Your rod and Your staff, they comfort me. You prepare a table before me in the presence of my enemies. You anoint my head with oil; my cup overflows. Surely Your goodness and love will follow me all the days of my life, and I will dwell in the house of the Lord forever.

Have you trusted Christ as your savior? Wouldn't it be nice to tell others about salvation through faith in Christ!

Our Destiny

While sitting at the park
Watching the people go by,
I wonder about each of them
And my heart gives out a sigh.

I wonder about their destiny
And if they're heaven bound,
In Christ's eternal book of life,
Will their names be found?

It's passing through this brief life
That each of us must decide
Where we will spend eternity,
And will we with Christ abide?

Christ died on the cross for all
And paid for everyone's sin,
Putting our trust in Him through faith
A new life can now begin.

So, as I watch the people pass
For each of them I'll pray,
That they'll trust Christ as their Savior
And we'll meet in heaven one day.

"How, then, can they call on the One they have not believed in? And how can they believe in the One of whom they have not heard? And how can they hear without someone preaching to them? And how can anyone preach unless they are sent? As it is written: 'How beautiful are the feet of those who bring good news.'" Romans 10:14,15

The Christian Walk

The Christian life is a walk with the Lord
Who is with us throughout our day,
He is not someone who we leave behind
Because then from His Word we will stray.

The Christian life is a walk with the Lord,
We are to be Ambassadors for Him
While preaching and teaching to all mankind,
Praising the Lord through prayer and hymn.

The Christian life is a walk with the Lord
While we are helping others in their need,
Which will bring blessings from God up above
As we serve Him in our thoughts and deed.

The Christian life is a walk with the Lord
Where we find fellowship and God's good grace,
When this life is through and we pass to glory,
We'll gaze with joy into our Savior's face.

Won't you trust Christ as your Savior now, so
that you can spend eternity with Him?

"Who shall separate us from the love of Christ: Shall trouble or hardship or persecution or famine or nakedness or danger or sword?... For I am convinced that neigher death nor life, neither angels nor demons, neither the present nor the future, nor any powers, neither height nor depth, nor anything else in all creation, will be able to separate us from the love of God that is in Christ Jesus our Lord."
Romans 8:35,38,39

God speaks to us through His Bible and through nature. Being out in nature is awesome and relaxing and shows us the handiwork of God. The Bible speaks about how God created the heavens and earth, and He created them for us to enjoy.

God gave us the Bible so that we can learn about Him and His will for our lives. It also speaks about how we are all sinners beginning with Adam and Eve.

We have all sinned and we cannot get into heaven with sin on us. Some people think that reading the Bible, praying, doing nice deeds will earn them eternal life. But that is not what the Bible teaches.

Praying and reading the Bible are good things to do, but being good does not take our sins away. If we could be good and go to heaven, then Christ would not have had to die on the cross for our sins.

Jesus came to earth to die on the cross for our sins in our place. Salvation is a free gift of God by trusting in the payment that Christ made on the cross. When you trust Jesus as your Savior, as a free gift, you can spend eternity with Christ.

If you haven't already, please thrust Christ as your Savior today!

If you would like more information, please contact me at:

sandybohonlmhc@gmail.com
www.sandybohonlmhc.com

Made in the USA
Middletown, DE
11 April 2024

52789292R00017